THOUGHTS FOR ASSOCIATIONS

Mark E. Frels, CAE (Ret.)

authorHOUSE

AuthorHouse™
1663 Liberty Drive
Bloomington, IN 47403
www.authorhouse.com
Phone: 1 (800) 839-8640

© 2019 Mark E. Frels, CAE (Ret.). All rights reserved.

No part of this book may be reproduced, stored in a retrieval system, or transmitted by any means without the written permission of the author.

Published by AuthorHouse 06/20/2019

ISBN: 978-1-7283-1605-5 (sc)
ISBN: 978-1-7283-1606-2 (hc)
ISBN: 978-1-7283-1607-9 (e)

Library of Congress Control Number: 2019907746

Print information available on the last page.

Any people depicted in stock imagery provided by Getty Images are models, and such images are being used for illustrative purposes only.
Certain stock imagery © Getty Images.

This book is printed on acid-free paper.

Because of the dynamic nature of the Internet, any web addresses or links contained in this book may have changed since publication and may no longer be valid. The views expressed in this work are solely those of the author and do not necessarily reflect the views of the publisher, and the publisher hereby disclaims any responsibility for them.

To the leaders and members of the Knox County Farm Bureau in Galesburg, Illinois, where it was my honor and privilege to begin my association-management career with dedicated, talented people engaged in that association to serve members and agriculture.

To Rolland W. "Mac" McKie, who served the Illinois Farm Bureau as a County Farm Bureau manager and a district director of field services, a position known today as regional manager. Mac was a gentleman, great mentor, colleague, and friend. He was an inspiration and role model to all who knew him.

Contents

Introduction ix

Chapter 1	Considering Association Programs—New and Existing	 1
Chapter 2	Mentoring	9
Chapter 3	Focusing on Employee Motivation	17
Chapter 4	Member Involvement	31
Chapter 5	The Reality of Membership Drives	41
Chapter 6	Communicating Effectively with People—Just Thoughts	57
Chapter 7	Dedication	69
Chapter 8	So You Want to Be a Leader	79

About the Author 91

Introduction

This is the third short, fundamental association-management book by Mark E. Frels. Topics covered in this book were not previously covered in his first two publications, *Just Common Sense* and *More Common Sense*. Those books deal with a variety of association-management topics on a very fundamental basis. This book deals with several specific association-management topics relevant to staff and leadership.

As stated in Mark's other publications, association-management techniques are both different from and similar to traditional corporate-management techniques. This book includes commentary pertaining to mentoring, the evaluation of existing and new association programming, employee motivation, member-involvement techniques, membership drives, working with people, and other subjects. As with other publications by this author, the reader will note the author embraces technology but also reminds us of the important need for teamwork and personal contact for associations to be successful. Further, the reader will note that the author once again stresses the need for complete and accurate communications for any and all association-management efforts to be successful.

As stated, the book is designed to be fundamental in nature and cause the reader to consider his or her actions on a daily basis in association management. As with Mark's other books, if the book contents stir the reader's thoughts, the book has achieved its goals.

Most important is for us to be successful in our association-management work as staff or leaders. Enjoy the book.

Chapter 1

Considering Association Programs—New and Existing

Membership associations have as their first and foremost objective the obvious goal to present programs and activities that meet the needs of the members. This makes perfect sense and should be a priority, and a measuring stick, before any existing program is continued or a new program is developed. Existing (even long-term, established) programs still should meet certain basic criteria in order to remain viable and continue.

From time to time, new programs should be developed to meet the changing needs of the membership, and perhaps existing programs need to be revised, eliminated, or replaced due to those same changing needs. Change is an extremely difficult concept for human beings. In the membership-association world, if we are to meet the continually changing needs of members, it is imperative we develop new programs, but we must also be bold enough to revise or eliminate long-term, existing programs or activities that no longer meet the needs of the members. Make sense? Yes. But it can be very hard to do!

As we look forward to developing a new program or deciding whether to revise or eliminate an existing program in favor of the new one, we need to utilize specific concepts and thought processes.

First, with new program development or analysis of an existing program, we must ask, "What is the goal of the program in terms of meeting members' needs and providing members value?" Perhaps better put, what is the purpose of the program, and why are we considering this new program? Or why was this program developed many years ago, and is it still relevant to our mission?

Often, a strategic planning process can lead an association board and staff down a road of accurate analysis regarding new program

development and evaluation of current programs. Oftentimes, in that strategic development process, it becomes quite clear which programs should remain, which programs should be eliminated, and where new program development is needed. However, the challenge with any strategic planning process is always the implementation of results. During a strategic planning process, we can develop a mission statement and analyze programs that fit under key desired result areas and then develop action plans to develop programs, and so forth. But the real challenge is the implementation of results. In other words, after the strategic planning process is completed, do we have enough courage to commit budget dollars in the right places, based on our planning analysis and best judgment? Are we brave enough to eliminate an established, long-term program that is still popular to a few but no longer serves the needs of most members?

These decisions are not easily made, especially in a membership association where we tend to really value (and for good reasons) the opinions and desires of each individual member.

So while a strategic planning process may be utilized to facilitate new program development and analyze the future of existing programs, we need to consider fundamental questions and criteria that any new program or existing program should meet. These include the following:

- Is the goal or purpose of the program or activity in keeping with the mission of the organization?
- Is the program relevant to board-determined priorities for the organization?
- Does the new program or existing program utilize budget dollars in a prudent manner in the best interest of the membership?
- What is the shelf life of the program? Is it apparent the program could have a long shelf life serving members? Or is the program being developed because of a specific and unique situation that just arose? And if that's the case, is action valid? It could be valid for the short term, the long term, or not at all.
- What are the realities of board and staff in being able to manage the new program or revise an existing program? In other words, does the organization have the expertise and resources to correctly facilitate the new program or the revisions of an existing program? Are other changes needed to facilitate?
- In the case of a new program, can or should the new program replace an existing program that may not be needed and better utilize budget dollars?

These and other questions need to be answered as we consider association programming and spending association dollars. It is also important to understand the budgeting aspects of program development pertaining to new and existing programs. When we attach budget dollars to any new program or existing program changes, we are making a statement that these programs make sense and are a priority. The fiduciary responsibility of the board (and staff for that matter) is to make sure this is the case. This is where a strategic planning process has value, because it causes the board and staff to take a formalized, step-by-step look at new program possibilities and existing programs through discussion and deliberation, which is healthy. When we commit valuable, limited budget dollars, it is important to understand that any program must be efficient and of value. The definition of *efficient* is the good use of budget dollars, including material resources and staff resources.

After the new program or the revised program is implemented, it is also important to evaluate the program at three months, six months, and a year later to see whether it is operating correctly or needs adjustments. Far too often, with a new or revised existing program, once we put it in place, we let it sit there for ten years or more. We need to do program review on at least a biannual basis after the first year. This is something the staff can be charged with facilitating, including presenting information to the board of directors. Or perhaps the analysis can be conducted by a committee of board members and staff—or really any way the association desires. The main point is to take a look, in whatever fashion the association determines is appropriate, at the new and existing programs to determine whether they remain relevant and of value and are functioning correctly.

Are we bold enough and dedicated enough to continually conduct this analysis? Remember: membership associations (generally speaking) don't like to eliminate programs—especially long-term programs. Therefore, quite often the enemy of efficiency, relevance, and the wise use of budget dollars can be change.

So let's move forward and think about further steps for considering a new or existing program.

Where did the idea come from? What are the reasons for the program and, therefore, the objectives? As we move forward in this consideration, we get into mechanical or action considerations that must be part of the process of analysis. As an example, what are the program needs from a capital expenditure standpoint? Is there specific equipment needed, and what is the life expectancy of that equipment? What is the anticipated cash outlay for that equipment? What are the staffing implications? This is one we always need to consider because, of course, staff time is money. Staff time has a significant cost in human resources, so we must ask whether existing staff can absorb a new program or activity or whether it will be necessary to add staff or reassign staff.

We need to take a realistic look at staff and leadership workloads and what a new program or revised activity would add to those workloads. We must provide leadership and staff with an opportunity to be successful with a new program. If they are completely overloaded before ever receiving the new assignment, the assignment can fail. Therefore, as we analyze a new program or revised activity, what are the cost factors for the first year of implementation and future years to be successful? All aspects of costs need to be considered as we analyze the viability of a program. If it is decided to proceed, then it is extremely important this program be included in the regular budget-approval process. Making the new program or activity part of the regular budget process is not only necessary to approve funds but also guarantees an ongoing, normal process of analysis and review of the program.

Another aspect of new or revised program consideration is whether or not there may be any return on investment. Does the program only have cost or expenditure factors, or is there revenue potential to help offset expenses of operating the program? This is another reason why it is important for the program to be included in the regular, normal budget process.

This chapter has outlined basic thoughts for developing new programs or for the evaluation of programs. It will be incumbent upon staff to prepare information for new or revised program development, as requested by the board of directors, to cover all these areas in anticipation of questions as the board proceeds through the phases of approval in the budget process. Obviously, and as always, the approval of any program or activity in a membership association rests with the board of directors, with the staff providing information as requested or bringing forward a new program for consideration. The board always has approval of the budget, including new or revised programs, new expenditures, additional staff, and hiring.

There is a lot to consider when you think about eliminating, revising, or creating programs, but maybe the most important thing to leave you with in this chapter is the following question: after you have conducted your strategic planning and answered these programming questions, if needed, can you implement change for the reasons outlined in this chapter?

Chapter 2

Mentoring

Mentoring: what does it mean? We often hear about association or company programs whereby a mentoring program is offered. Probably the first thing that comes to most people's minds (which makes sense) is something like a coaching program. In other words, someone will be assigned to work with another individual to learn and further develop their professional growth. Over the years, mentoring programs have gained in popularity, with good reason.

Probably the best and most common form of a mentoring program is an internship. What better way to coach an individual and further develop their professional skills than through actual day-to-day experience? This also allows the association an opportunity to monitor the professional growth of the individual while assessing them for a future position. There is nothing like experience. The purpose of any mentoring program is to seek out potentially excellent employees and engage them in an intern or mentoring program to facilitate further growth for the benefit of that individual(s) and the association. These are the most common, basic concepts anyone thinks of when they think of a mentoring program. Let's consider some more specific questions or concepts.

We can probably agree that *mentoring* means preparing someone through training and experience for a specific position or assignment. As part of that process, it certainly means challenging the individual to discover skills they are proficient at and those skills needing further development, as well as to assess preparedness for a future position or assignment.

The mentoring process offers an evaluation opportunity. This opportunity provides the individual and the association with the benefits of a performance review for the individual both during and at the conclusion of the mentoring process. This allows recommendations to be made for professional development, and an assessment can be made on the progress of the individual. Actually, a mentoring program should involve an assessment of an individual at the beginning, midpoint, and conclusion of the mentoring program to see whether progress has been achieved. This helps to determine the road map for future professional development of the individual. A mentoring program (or an internship program) provides a unique advantage. That advantage is day-to-day practical experience, which the employee will be engaged in with supervisors and other employees.

The assessment of skills and mechanics needed to succeed are definitely a very important part of a mentoring program. There are all types of training functions and activities that can be put in place to develop these skills for an employee. There are also more subjective assessments that need to be included in any mentoring program. The individual involved in a mentoring program should be provided with challenges and assignments that test not only those mechanical skill sets (such as speaking, writing, etc.) but also judgment abilities in a variety of low- and higher-pressure situations. If we are going to assess individuals for promotions or future positions, it is important that we understand the judgment and reasoning abilities of the individual. This includes common sense, ethics, drive, and so on. These are extremely important factors that need to be judged and considered as part of any mentoring program.

A more subjective area, which must also be addressed, is a general analysis of the individual's leadership characteristics. I just mentioned judgment, and certainly judgment is a huge leadership characteristic, but judgment is so important that it should stand on its own. Another leadership characteristic is the ability to communicate clearly, properly, and effectively with employees and leadership. It also includes the ability to collaborate effectively with other employees and, if assigned, to lead. Does the individual have the ability to effectively lead a team and, in that process, delegate authority in such a manner to bring out the best talents of those individuals for the overall achievement of the team, while accurately explaining the mission of an assignment to the group? Does the individual have the ability to allow team members that he or she may supervise the freedom to operate, create, and be productive, while maintaining a reporting structure back to the individual in charge in a supervisory capacity? Make no mistake about it: we all know that is a skill.

These characteristics have a great deal to do with that often-mysterious item called personality. Does the individual possess the right personality to lead and motivate people? Do other employees want to be part of the team that this individual will head? As we review the needed characteristics of an individual, we need to consider collaboration, motivation, judgment, ethics, and also fairness and team leadership. These are just a few, and there are more, but these are some of the core basic characteristics that need to be analyzed in a mentoring program.

Coordinating with these characteristics, and going along with personality, is another subjective word that supervisors sometimes find very difficult to deal with. That word is *attitude*. Does the individual in the program possess a winning attitude? Does that sound trite? I submit to you that it is not. We all have hard days and better days at work, but does this individual possess an attitude that allows them to be a positive influence on other employees? Attitude is extremely important and a huge part of any leadership analysis.

As we move forward and evaluate an individual at the conclusion of a mentoring program, it is very important to keep notes. These subjects must be documented, and if performance discussions are held at the beginning, midpoint, and end, that documentation, targeting specific areas where an individual needs to improve, will be mandatory. The value of a mentoring program is to do exactly this: develop a list of strengths and weaknesses and then move forward to facilitate employee development if deemed appropriate.

At the conclusion of any mentoring program (intern or existing employee), it could be extremely important (as the individual is considered for employment or a promotion) to construct an individual development plan for the person. I have covered this subject at length in other books. The development of an individual development plan, as outlined in my other books, *Just Common Sense* and *More Common Sense*, could be exactly the correct tool for a supervisor to utilize at the conclusion of a mentoring program to facilitate further employee professional development.

So, at the heart of a mentoring program, is it really just a training program? Well, we might say it's a training program and a comprehensive employee developmental and discovery program. The mentoring program allows a new employee or an existing or possible new employee to be coached by a more experienced and successful employee. The mentoring program provides an opportunity for the company to discover the strengths, weaknesses, and characteristics of an individual, and for the individual to discover these for himself or herself as well. People often view a mentoring program as one-sided, meaning just an opportunity for the company to consider an individual, and while this is important, it is also an opportunity for discovery by the individual themselves.

So, let's do a quick bullet point review:

- Mentoring is a training program but also a learning opportunity that could be best followed by an individual development plan if the company and individual are interested in future employment opportunities.
- A mentoring program is designed to prepare a person for a future position or assignment through day-to-day practical experience, including discovery of strengths and weaknesses and how to address those issues.

- One of the aspects of any mentoring program should be challenging the individual in both their comfort zone and non-comfort zone areas, allowing them to further develop and discover skills and preparedness for future assignments.
- The mentoring program should include an assessment at the beginning and a performance review at midpoint and end. If it is determined the employee is to move forward with the association, then an individual development plan could follow the last performance review and be part of the employee's plans for continuing professional development.
- The assessment of an individual's judgment is paramount in the mentoring process. The individual should be presented with scenarios and assignments designed to challenge and test their judgment.
- An individual involved in a mentoring program should receive assignments designed to test their ability to collaborate with employees, lead, and bring out the best in other employees. Strengths and weaknesses in these regards should be noted and discussed for possible inclusion in future learning.
- The individual's attitude must be assessed as well. The positive daily attitude of the individual is of paramount importance.

We have talked almost exclusively about mentoring specifically addressing the individual being trained or challenged. I also want to concentrate on another important point. We must always first consider the role of the mentor. He or she must possess an outstanding record; have excellent judgment and skills; have an excellent attitude; and have a reputation within the association that is outstanding—or that individual should not be a mentor. The biggest disaster for any

Thoughts for Associations

mentoring program occurs if the mentor does not coach or mentor properly. It is extremely important that the mentor have a great attitude about the association and possess the skills and ethics necessary to correctly fill the mentor role. Mentors have a tremendous impact on employees, and often after the employee completes the mentoring program, that employee will continue to rely on that mentor for advice and counsel in situations or, perhaps, instead of or in addition to his or her supervisor. This is why choosing a mentor is so critically important and must be done carefully. It is certainly understandable, especially in the cases of younger employees who are mentoring with an experienced employee, that they would and should see their mentor as a role model. Why would they not? The company or the association has designated this individual as a mentor, so, certainly, the company has made the statement that this person is a role model for other employees. Therefore, before someone is named a mentor, they should be a role model for other employees in every sense of the word, or they should not be in the mentoring program.

Mentoring programs, whether via an internship program or another approach, can have great value for the association and the participating individual if properly conducted.

Chapter 3

Focusing on Employee Motivation

Employee motivation may seem like a subjective topic, and it certainly does have many subjective characteristics. The ability of a supervisor to motivate an employee to bring out his or her best work depends on the personality and skills of the supervisor and the attitude they bring to work each day.

There are certain keys that lead a supervisor to successfully motivate an employee. Some of these are subjective by nature, and some are not. Some are more tangible, such as compensation. Let's start by considering some of the major keys to successfully motivating an employee and then go back and analyze those specific keys with a detailed approach. Among the major keys to motivating an employee is expressing belief in the employee. The supervisor must express belief in the talents and abilities of the employee. The supervisor must empower the employee to carry out duties and assignments with the employee understanding the supervisor has confidence in his or her actions. However, that empowerment must certainly carry reporting provisions with it. That is, parameters for the employee to operate within, and, certainly, the employee must report back to the supervisor, with the supervisor having ultimate control over whatever the project or assignments may be. There is an important message a supervisor sends to an employee when they empower that employee to make decisions within parameters. This message carries with it a responsibility the employee must embrace to both move forward and also keep the supervisor informed. Very good judgment on behalf of the employee is needed and will be tested.

The next key to the motivation of an employee is mutual respect. There must be mutual respect between the supervisor and employee. There must be a shared integrity between the supervisor and employee if the supervisor is to successfully motivate that employee to move forward in assigned areas and succeed. This requires professionalism and maturity.

Another key to motivation is showing and receiving appreciation. It is important for the supervisor to show appreciation to the employee when appropriate, and, likewise, the employee has an obligation to return appreciation to the supervisor, when appropriate, for supervision and guidance that has led to success. Never underestimate the importance of showing appreciation to someone. I have always operated under the rule that if something needs to be corrected, the best thing to do is correct it immediately, especially in regard to employee attitude or performance. If difficult tasks must be handled, they should be handled as quickly as reasonably possible within the parameters of good judgment and procedures. Likewise, and just as important, is the fact that appreciation should be shown to someone who does a good job and has excelled at an assignment or moved into new areas successfully. This assignment belongs to the supervisor in terms of recognizing the employee, but it is also important for an employee to show appreciation to the supervisor for the learning and mentoring they are receiving.

The next key area so important to motivation is rewards. A lot of people will tell you the only reward that matters is monetary. Those same people will tell you that a promotion is not a promotion unless it involves a raise, meaning more compensation or benefits. To be sure, and without question, monetary reward is extremely important. If an employee accepts increased assignments or takes a new position or has earned additional compensation through some outstanding effort, then monetary reward is, of course, appropriate. Monetary reward is most likely what we are all the most familiar with because of bonus programs (that have certain parameters) or because of annual performance reviews where salary and compensation packages are reviewed. However, rewards don't only come in a monetary fashion. Rewards can come in the form of other actions, which we will discuss further. For now, let us first remember that rewarding someone is an important part of motivation. It is a huge part of human nature to desire to be recognized and rewarded.

Another important key to successful motivation is the role of the supervisor as a role model. In order for a supervisor to successfully motivate an employee, the employee must see that supervisor as a role model. Earlier, I spoke about one aspect of this, because mutual respect is so important. When we return to this subject, we will analyze a variety of ways a supervisor can be a role model. If, as a supervisor, the employee you are trying to motivate does not see you as a role model, it will make the task of motivation extremely difficult.

Mark E. Frels, CAE (Ret.)

The supervisor must allow the employee to learn from constructive mistakes. Please note the term *constructive mistakes*, which we will analyze in more detail later. Of course, constructive mistakes means learning from mistakes that provide a benefit to the employee as he or she gains experience. It does not mean letting an employee fall in a hole so deep they can never recover. But the employee you are trying to motivate must be allowed to try things on their own and make constructive mistakes in order to learn.

Fundamental to the process of motivating an employee and fundamental to the process of anything we do (this will surprise none of you that have read my books) is communication. In order for there to be a successful relationship between a supervisor and an employee, there must be excellent, clear, understood communication.

So, let's recap each of the key areas for motivation of an employee that we have raised and can now analyze in more detail:

- supervisor belief in the employee
- the supervisor empowering the employee with parameters
- mutual respect
- showing and receiving appreciation

- rewards
- the supervisor being a role model
- making constructive mistakes
- communications

As we look to cover more detailed information about each of these key areas that contribute to the motivation of an employee, let's start with some comments about expressing belief in the employee. When a supervisor and an employee sit down to discuss assignments, it is important for the supervisor to be positive with the employee. The supervisor must take the lead in expressing sincere belief in the employee regarding his or her abilities for the tasks and assignments that are going to be put before that employee. If those tasks or assignments may lead to a promotion, this should be discussed up front, although we know (that most often) guarantees cannot be made or should not be made. It is important for the supervisor to specifically cover expectations for the employee. It is difficult for an employee to be motivated and move forward successfully if the supervisor is vague about expectations. The supervisor not only has to express sincere belief in the employee's abilities but also has to be specific in explaining what the duties and tasks are in front of the employee. As part of that explanation, the supervisor also must explain how success will be measured. How will the employee know if he or she has been successful? What is the impact expected from the assignments the employee is being asked to carry out? The supervisor must explain each assignment's value and what the objectives are of those assignments. In addition, without making guarantees (which is often difficult, especially in corporate environments with conditions that can change on a regular basis), the supervisor must explain what the benefits are to the employee of successfully meeting his or her goals. This may be a bonus, or it could be an opportunity for a new assignment that is of interest to the employee, or recognition, whatever may be appropriate. To be fair to the supervisor and the organization, the employee must also understand what happens if he or she fails. However, that should initially be kept to a minimum part of the discussion, at least in the beginning, because the whole purpose is to motivate the employee in a positive fashion and help them move forward understanding that they have support of the organization and their supervisor.

In regard to empowering with parameters, this means exactly what is stated. It is important for the supervisor to empower the employee. The employee we want to motivate must understand they have a certain amount of authority to operate within certain parameters on a given assignment or task. They need to know they can make some decisions and, of course, that they will be held accountable. This can be just as difficult for the supervisor as the employee. The employee must clearly understand these parameters so he or she can operate correctly and not get out of bounds with regard to the chain of command and reporting. The supervisor can encounter just as much difficulty with this assignment as the employee. For this to work correctly, the supervisor must give up some control of the project or task for the employee to learn and develop. This is one of those areas that can be as big a challenge for the supervisor as the employee. It is important they work together on this. A frank discussion about empowerment with parameters between the supervisor and the employee is crucial to the motivation of the employee and their relationship. Nothing will cause an employee to become more disgruntled than being held accountable to carry out certain tasks or functions and then not be given any opportunity to operate or function using their own judgment. How else can they grow and develop? Also, allowing that employee to have some empowerment increases the opportunity of the supervisor to further mentor the employee. As the employee has questions and naturally grows through this process, this empowerment stimulates further discussion between the employee and the supervisor, increasing the mutual respect between those individuals. The supervisor that allows the employee some empowerment within parameters will also grow further a supervisor and as a mentor. Therefore, in the mentoring process, the supervisor and the employee must have a clear, frank discussion about what kind of empowerment the employee has with any new project or assignment and what kind of authority parameters exist.

Thoughts for Associations

The supervisor and the employee must also have genuine mutual respect, specifically for the opinions but also for the judgment that each brings to the table. Respect of judgment is so important in overall mutual respect. There is also a level of maturity that is required by both, and this must be a characteristic both the supervisor and the employee possess. As an example, there are going to be times when the supervisor and the employee do not agree, and there must be an understanding that this is not personal. Oftentimes, people have a difficult time understanding this. In order for mutual respect to exist and genuinely be held between the two parties, it must be understood that when a supervisor disagrees with an employee or vice versa, it is business and not personal. Holding of grudges should not be allowed, and that is extremely difficult for some people. There also needs to be complete understanding that if there is disagreement having to do with program development or a task, the supervisor wins. The employee needs to understand that the supervisor is still the supervisor. The employee needs to respect the experience and abilities of the supervisor, and the supervisor must respect the ambition, talents, and abilities of the employee if the two are to function in a cohesive manner that allows the employee to receive proper mentoring and, therefore, learn and professionally develop. This discussion between the supervisor and the employee, regarding mutual respect, must occur early in the mentoring process.

Showing and receiving appreciation. Once again, those of you who have read my other association-management books know how I feel about showing and receiving appreciation. It is usually not done often enough and is extremely important. The nature of human beings is such that most of us like to be recognized, and we want to receive approval for what we are doing. As a matter of fact, this—possibly above any other action—is what keeps us moving forward. We may not always admit that, but I think it is important and true.

The supervisor always has an obligation to show appreciation. This can be done privately or in public. By public, you understand that I mean in a company meeting or at some kind of a function in front of a larger body of people. It is important that recognition be done in a manner appropriate to the task being recognized. In other words, the showing of appreciation should fit what we are appreciating. There are times when a thank-you note is appropriate and nothing more is needed. There are times when more is needed.

There is also another aspect of recognition that supervisors always need to consider, and that is how the recognition will be received by other employees. In other words, recognition should not be given unless it is deserved. Supervisors need to understand that recognizing a specific individual also provides motivation to other employees and holds that individual up as an example. If for some reason, other employees see the recognition as not deserved, not only will the recognition be useless to the employee receiving it, but it will have exactly the opposite effect as it should on other employees. It is incumbent upon supervisors to make sure recognition is given only when deserved. It is also incumbent upon supervisors to make sure everyone is recognized who should be recognized. A supervisor should obviously not recognize a five-person team by singling out only two people. Now, you say to yourself, "Who would do that?" It happens. As important as recognition is, supervisors need to make sure the recognition fits the deed and is appropriate, not only in the best interest of the employee(s) receiving the recognition and the association but also in the best interest of the other employees.

It is also important for the employee or employees receiving the recognition to show appreciation for that recognition. This does not need to be overdone, but it certainly is appropriate for the employee who received recognition (especially in a public situation) to formally express thanks to the supervisor and company for the recognition. Courtesy is always the most appropriate approach, and operating professionally is always the key to success. Providing recognition or saying thank you may seem like subjects that would not need to be in a book, but they most certainly do. Far too often, I have heard a supervisor say, "We don't need to thank them for that. That's what they get paid for." That may be true, but it certainly does nothing for team building or motivating an individual or a group. The truth is motivation is key to the continued success for any employee or employee group, and recognition is paramount to that motivation.

I mentioned earlier that another key area in motivating employees is rewards. One might say that my commentary on showing appreciation or recognition is a form of reward, and that is true. So, let's assume we've already covered that one. Rewards come in a wide variety of forms. Some people want to receive a plaque or a trophy they can hang on their wall, other people want a bigger office with a window, other people want a couch in their office, and somebody else wants more vacation time. Everybody is different in their definition or expectation of what a reward may be for a job well done. Certainly, as I mentioned earlier, most people think of a reward as monetary, and that is understandable. Honestly, few things drive people more than receiving more compensation.

Another specific area most people would say provides a reward is a promotion, and, of course, with a promotion often comes increased compensation. So, we can talk about rewards as monetary, receiving a promotion, or maybe other areas as well. This all depends on the desires of the individual and the approach of the human resources professionals and management professionals in the organization or company. We need to understand that reward can come in a lot of different forms. I would offer the suggestion that in the performance-review process, there should be an opportunity (as I mentioned in one of my other books) for the employee and the supervisor to talk about future desires of the employee. This may be a promotion or a lateral movement to another job that interests the employee. This could be the implementation of an individual development plan for the professional growth and development of an employee. It could be the interest of the employee in a specific job or a variety of other things. During that performance-review process, it is quite possible that the discussion could include what types of rewards could possibly motivate the employee the most. Throughout my career, I had this discussion with some employees who said that what motivated them the most was that they wanted my job. That is certainly not something I ever took offense to. As a matter of fact, I always thought it was probably a very honest answer. That led us, usually, into a discussion about an individual development plan or training assignments for that employee, if appropriate. An employee who told me they were motivated by the prospect of possibly getting my job someday was hopefully telling me they were interested in additional compensation, of course, but also in a promotion and more responsibility, and that they were willing to dedicate even more of themselves to the company or organization, including effort and time, as well as other factors. That answer is a tremendous answer, but it carries with it a lot of responsibility.

As supervisors strive to motivate employees, it is important during the performance-review process, or whenever a supervisor and employee have a private discussion, that they talk about what rewards would motivate the employee. It's not always going to be a promotion or monetary. I have had conversations with excellent employees who did not want a promotion and who were very happy with the compensation package they had, but what they desired the most was some kind of flexible working hours or more vacation time to spend with family, and subjects of that nature. Sometimes we make an assumption that everybody wants to be promoted, and while a lot of people desire promotions, not everyone wants to be promoted. One of my challenges as a supervisor has been working with an employee who had tremendous potential but knowing that employee did not desire to advance further in the organization. As a supervisor, I had a responsibility to challenge the employee's thinking in that regard, but ultimately, the decision is, of course, up to the employee. Again, what is the nature of reward that motivates a specific employee? That's a great discussion, given all these thoughts and comments, for a supervisor and an employee to have.

Moving on to mutual respect, there must be mutual respect between supervisor and employee. A good supervisor, as a good mentor, should challenge certain things and be willing to correct certain actions of the employee they are mentoring. The supervisor, as a mentor, does this in the best interest of his or her employees and the company, and that positive attitude always shows through every single day, regardless of what is happening. I had a saying at one time that people found interesting: "There are no problems; there are only situations that need correct addressing and resolution." I always found that to be true.

It means exactly what you might think it means: if a problem exists, fix it the best way possible. Let's face it, a supervisor should not let an employee totally fail at something or, shall we say, fall in a hole they can never dig out of. But it is important to allow an employee to exercise his or her judgment, and if a supervisor knows this may lead to a problem or a mistake, the supervisor needs to decide whether he or she should step in and stop that action or let the employee learn from it. It is often important to let the employee learn from their mistakes. As a matter of fact, the supervisor can take a hybrid approach to this. For example, I have been in mentoring situations where an employee wanted to do something and I knew it was a mistake, but I also knew it would not be devastating or have a lasting impact. Sometimes I allowed the employee to proceed in those situations, and when things didn't go exactly the way the employee thought they would, we had great discussion material. Sometimes I even took a more proactive approach to this and told the employee in the beginning what I thought would happen if they proceeded with actions they were proposing. Sometimes in those situations, I still allowed the employee to proceed, and when things didn't go well, we again had great discussion material. As a supervisor, I certainly did not say to the employee, when the mistake occurred, "I told you so." That is not the approach I took. The approach I took was to have a frank discussion with the employee about what happened and what was learned from the situation, and we then moved forward. It is incumbent upon the supervisor to handle this in the right way. Jumping up and down at a new or existing employee and saying "I told you so" does not help the employee-employer relationship. Allowing an employee to make constructive mistakes that he or she can learn from has value. The supervisor, however, also needs to make sure, if he or she uses this approach, that whatever actions may or may not occur do not damage or cause great difficulties to the company or other employees. In other words, the supervisor has to use his or her own good judgment about mistakes they allow the employee to learn from. So much of this is subjective but has value if handled correctly and if people proceed in a mature, professional, learning environment. By that I mean, if the supervisor and the employee refrain from taking these issues personally and have the kind of mutual respect that allows them to move forward in a productive manner (with the end result being the employee learning), then mutual respect and progress will be realized.

Let me conclude this chapter by again saying that communication is of paramount importance between the supervisor and the employee. Regular communication must be established to discuss how things are going and answer questions the employee may have, or to provide the supervisor coaching opportunities, which are so very important. Employees should prepare for that communication by making a list and being ready to ask questions so they can get answers in an efficient manner from the supervisor. Likewise, the supervisor should be prepared with notes before any discussion, regarding comments they want to make or questions they want to ask the employee. If a supervisor is to be successful, and if an employee is to be successful, it is absolutely inexcusable for either party to consider not having time to communicate. Communication is the foundation of all successful endeavors, as I have said on many occasions.

Chapter 4

Member Involvement

It should be obvious nothing is more vital to any membership association than member involvement. The involvement of members is vital to operations and imperative for the development of leaders. In order to be successful, member involvement also has to be generational. The younger generation coming forward is, indeed, the future of the association. We have all heard that said about associations over time, whether it be a club we belong to, a church, or any other organization.

As we understand the need for member involvement and leadership development, it becomes important to define what member involvement means. For our purposes, we could start with this definition: investment by an individual of their time, energy, and talents in the causes and purposes of the association. At least that would be the definition that makes the most sense to me.

There is nothing more valuable to any of us than time and energy, and most associations usually ask for time and energy (as well as funding, of course) from their members and leaders. To say our society has changed greatly over the last several years would be a gross understatement. There have been huge changes in the way we function at home, including how the family unit functions, and in the workforce. Workplace environments

Mark E. Frels, CAE (Ret.)

have changed, along with other employment factors, and it will continue to have a tremendous impact on volunteer member involvement.

In order for associations to thrive, it will be extremely important to continue our analysis of what member involvement means and adapt to changes. By the same token, there are some old-school member-involvement techniques that should survive as well, in compatibility with new approaches and techniques, so we remain effective and connected with one another in a world that is ever changing. Remember, associations exist to connect people interested in like causes and to accomplish efforts together.

The definition of member involvement continues to evolve. Let's take a look at the family first. The most obvious change affecting member involvement in any organization, school activity, or church activity is the change in the family unit. Both mom and dad work outside the home, and this is necessary to make ends meet and for any hope of increasing disposable income to enjoy a better quality of life. That change probably has the most impact on member involvement. People are not as willing to attend meetings and travel on the weekends or during the week if they have free time.

The next most obvious change over the last thirty to forty years that has affected member involvement is in technology. Everyone has a smartphone, and now we can wear them on our wrist—just like those of you who are old enough to remember that image of Dick Tracey in the old comic book days. The young generation says, "Who?" However, that's the reality. We wear monitors reading our bodily functions, telling us what to eat, when to eat, how many steps we've taken, what our blood pressure and heart rate are, and everything else you can imagine. The speed with which we communicate is not just fast; it is immediate. This is expected by the current generation and will be by future generations. The way we are entertained is totally impacted by technology. Entertainment is continuing to evolve, and the way we study, research, and learn will never be the same and will continue changing.

Associations must effectively use technology to define member involvement in the future, because future generations demand this. Involvement through technology must be embraced. But it remains important to meet people face-to-face and shake hands. We still need face-to-face conversations in accordance with work to be done and to foster the collaboration that must occur for a team to be effective in association management. This pertains to staff and leaders. We still need to get together from time to time. However, our society will never again tolerate holding meetings like we used to years ago. It is simply a time, cost, and efficiency question. We had meetings to plan meetings, and people were very glad to attend and were interested. However, all those factors I previously mentioned have changed and will continue to change.

Having said all of this obvious information leads me to the question I started this chapter with: as we look to the future and toward keeping our membership associations successful, how do we define member involvement?

First, there are certain characteristics of member involvement we need to consider. In order for members to want to be involved, they must see value in their involvement. This is a twofold analysis. They must feel that the valuable time and energy they invest benefits the organization and is also of benefit to them and their family. If members of an association do not feel there is value to their involvement, they will not be members or be involved very long. Later in this chapter, we will talk about targeted techniques to allow members to feel productive about their involvement and their investment of time and energy.

Involvement must also be efficient. In today's world, members will not remain if activities are not efficient. Members must feel that their time and energy are not only invested toward a good cause but are being utilized by the association in an efficient and successful manner. I also still believe association members today enjoy the social aspect of their involvement. I believe the social aspect of people getting together, collaborating, and discussing issues they share an interest in has great value. It is one of the factors members see as valuable. Having said that, there is a much higher expectation today that business meetings or work aspects of involvement in the association will not only be valuable but also managed efficiently. The last several generations have continued to develop an intolerance for what they call wasted time. The generations before them may not have viewed that time as wasted. Yet there is a high expectation today, which will continue, that work time should be managed efficiently and that social time in associations should be available to those interested but not forced on everyone. Today, members want to decide how much time they will spend socializing. They don't want the socializing mixed with work time. This is not to say an event sponsored by an association, such as a convention, should not and could not have social time and work time as well. However, I believe today's association member wants to see those time blocks segregated in a manner that allows them to choose where and when they will invest their time. This was not always the case in the past, but it seems evident this is highly desirable by people today.

Thoughts for Associations

Another key to member involvement today has to do with paying expenses. Given the financial pressures today and the changing world, I believe we have reached a point in the association world where paying expenses for association leaders is a must. By that, I mean if an association has the financial ability to do so, leaders and members should have expenses paid when they travel or conduct business on behalf of the association. Many associations do this already and have for some time. It is a fair approach. If a member is asked to travel on behalf of the association, it seems reasonable the association should not expect that financial burden to land on the member. This seems reasonable and appropriate and will go a long way in helping members feel good about being involved. The days of personally paying for expenses in most membership organizations are probably gone. There are exceptions, of course, with associations or organizations that are philanthropic or religious, for example. My purpose in this commentary is to focus on membership associations, trade associations, and so on, outside of those other specific areas. Having just made the statement about paying expenses for members working on behalf of the association, this raises another question. This is the question of per diem. If a membership association has the financial ability, it is also becoming more of an expectation that the association compensate a leader, in particular, or member working on behalf of the organization for his or her time. It is one thing to pay for travel expenses, but it is becoming more of an expectation that there should be some reasonable payment for the investment of a person's time and talent in the activities of the organization. My observation, when it comes to most organizations, has been that this approach may most often pertain to leaders who are investing considerable time, such as the president or officers of a board, or maybe in some cases committee chairs or others. Not too many years ago, this was not that common.

Another key concept to member involvement is the amount of time that we expect from members and leaders. Earlier in this chapter, I talked about the newer generation expecting their time would be used in an efficient manner. In order for members to stay involved, it continues to be an expectation that the amount of time a member needs to invest in the organization will be only the amount needed to correctly carry out the tasks being asked of that member. In other words, there is an expectation that through the use of technology, and simply as a philosophy and approach of the organization, the time requirement itself must be kept to what I would call a "correct minimum." It is expected that the time requirement must accurately match the assigned tasks and not go beyond that.

If possible, the amount of time needed for involvement by a member should be set by the member themselves, not dictated to them. Through alternative member-involvement structures being used today, this can be accomplished and can increase the base number of people involved in the association. It is to the advantage of the organization to have members engaged in activities that they feel have value and that they are passionate about and very interested in. Associations have not always considered those factors, and today, if we want members involved, we need to consider those concepts. There is great value in having a member choose the subject area or leadership position they want to be involved in. If we allow this, the member feels much better about time invested and will be more productive and happier serving the organization. We most enjoy things we are interested in. That's human nature, and membership associations need to understand the fundamental fact that this will increase member involvement, and members will be more passionate and productive on behalf of the association.

So, what does this mean? It means that member-involvement structures (formally most often called committees) should be creative, should be efficient in their use of time, should utilize technology to achieve that efficiency (both in terms of organization resources and member time), and should be subject-matter driven in fairly specific areas, allowing members to choose areas for involvement. There should not be meetings for the sake of having meetings. Meetings should still be held when needed, and there will definitely be times when meetings should be held so people can discuss issues eye to eye and shake hands. However, the days of meeting every month because "we have always met every month" are gone. An ideal system would be one whereby member-involvement task forces, councils, cabinets, or whatever title you choose to use, are formed on a subject-matter basis, with a chairman or leader, possibly from the association's board of directors, to lead that group. A great deal of work can be accomplished through the use of technology, with some meetings throughout the year. It would be even better if the group (or the member-involvement unit) had the ability to make decisions on how they wanted to conduct their business in accordance with how they felt about the use of time.

Mark E. Frels, CAE (Ret.)

I touched on something in the previous paragraph that I need to expand on at this time. This is a comment about the association's board of directors. As we move forward in our discussion about member involvement, it is important to remember that the association's board of directors, in accordance with the bylaws of the association, still needs to be in charge and have overall control of how member-involvement structures are facilitated, along with budgets and so on. The board still has the overall responsibility for staffing the organization and a fiduciary responsibility to the membership, which must be taken quite seriously. Perhaps, through a strategic-planning process or other methods, the board of directors can establish member-involvement structures and implement those in an effective manner. But make no mistake about it: the control of the organization, including structure, budget, staffing, and other factors, belongs to the association's board of directors in accordance with the bylaws and policies of the association. We don't want to lose sight of that because that formality remains extremely important in maintaining order and an association that functions correctly. Governance must always be understood and clearly in place.

We also don't want to limit member involvement. If we have members that want to be involved to a greater degree, it is important that we provide an opportunity for members to do so. I have witnessed some member-involvement structures that don't allow for this. For example, there is no reason for an association to make up its various subject-oriented task forces or committees only from members of the board, and not long ago, this was a common practice in some associations. I would encourage associations to open their member-involvement structures to their membership. No doubt there is a huge number of members with great expertise in a wide variety of different areas, some of whom may have interest in serving on a task force or a committee. Once again, I advocate control. The board of directors should have the final say about who serves on a task force or committee, but opening involvement opportunities to members provides more ownership to those members and shares the workload. That approach certainly taps the great expertise and knowledge that members no doubt possess and may desire to share with the association. Also, doing this encourages more member involvement. It is very important we provide members an opportunity to soar in areas they have a passion for and interest in, with regard to subject matter.

Let's discuss names for member-involvement structures. As long as those new member-involvement structures carry forth the characteristics that we have talked about in this chapter, it doesn't matter what you call them. For the sake of change, we could probably agree the word "committee" may be something we don't want to use anymore. If that word still works for your association, then so be it. Don't change it. However, other terminology includes task forces, action teams, councils, special forces, cabinet, unit, forum, brigade, and group. I know there are lots of other titles that can be used. Sometimes for the sake of change, there is value in coming up with a new name and new approach, especially if it really does reflect a change in the opportunity we define as member involvement. I also feel the more focused these member-involvement areas are, the more likely associations are to find members with a real passion for that specific area. For example, the organization I spent my career working with developed an Ag in the Classroom program. I was at the forefront of that development. This was a specific approach to teaching agricultural awareness through school curriculum to elementary school students. The opportunity to be specifically involved in this effort tremendously increased member involvement in that subject area and, therefore, in organization. This program has been incredibly successful. As a matter of fact, it has become a model in its subject area for the rest of the nation. This is an example of providing members with an opportunity for involvement in a specific area of interest to them. Sometimes our previous committee structures were so broad based and tried to do so much they struggled, and members became less than enthusiastic about being involved.

Let me provide some other ideas that many of you may already be using for subject matter for specific member-involvement structures. Some of these might be local government, state or national legislation, county board liaison work, land-use issues, leadership development, and more. You get the idea. Give these member-involvement structures any title you want, but this approach is valuable. As you consider your member-involvement structures, these are just some thoughts on how to take those efforts into the future successfully.

Perhaps very little of this is new, but you need to ask yourself if your association is utilizing the concepts. If you know about these concepts but are not implementing them (and are still doing things the old way) and wondering why nobody signs up for committees, then I suggest you change things. As I have said before, one of the biggest challenges humans have is the desire to not change. But I think as long as we change with a reasonable plan and, most importantly, with the right goals in mind (that is paramount), we can't go wrong. Challenge your own thinking and correctly challenge the association. Think seriously about member involvement and what that means. The organization it was my great privilege to work for has done this and offers lots of different member-involvement opportunities, and those member-involvement opportunities have been quite successful. The same can be true for your association or organization.

Chapter 5

The Reality of Membership Drives

Membership is essential to any association, especially volunteer-membership associations. How often have we heard "membership is the lifeblood of the organization?" That statement is s true not only for the collection of dues to financially support the organization but also regarding member involvement. Membership associations provide a variety of programs and services for members that can be achieved together through an association, which otherwise might not be possible. Membership associations bring people of like

interests together for the purpose of sharing ideas, developing services and programs, and establishing policies to benefit members. All the basic, standard stuff—right?

A membership drive gives new people an opportunity to join the organization to meet their needs and interests. It is important for membership associations to sponsor membership drives from time to time to sign new members, showcase the association's accomplishments, and bring further visibility to the association. In membership associations, we often underestimate the need to promote the association.

As we consider membership drives, we need to boldly, honestly understand the realities of conducting a membership drive. The truth is that most people, if honest, really don't like to participate in drives. There are always exceptions, but often people are uncomfortable asking someone to join an organization and pay dues. Most people don't like asking someone else for something, especially money and time. If you are going to ask someone to join an organization, you must be well prepared. The most common and expected questions are how much are the dues and "What do I get for my money?" Plain and simple. The other item that weighs heavily on most people's minds is "What kind of time commitment am I getting myself into?" These questions can make participating in a membership drive uncomfortable for some. People today are more conscious than ever about committing their money, time, and energy, especially with both spouses working and families involved in multiple commitments. These subjects make membership drives more challenging and make preparation even more important. Let's discuss how to approach these subjects and move forward in a positive manner.

Often, when going on a membership drive, when you arrive at someone's home, you already know what the person is thinking: *Here they come. What do they want?* That causes an uncomfortable feeling from the start, but again, we need to consider how to approach people. Let's review some of the following subjects:

- What are the legitimate challenges of a membership drive today?
- What is the human nature aspect of membership drives?
- Who are the best people to conduct a membership drive?
- What tools and preparations are needed before ever approaching a prospective member?

Our lives are more complex than ever before. In today's world, conducting a membership drive is more difficult than ever because, more than likely, both partners are involved in a full-time job, the kids are very involved in multiple activities, and most people today are involved with a significant amount of communication via social media. You might say the best way to conduct a

membership drive is through email or any of the numerous social media outlets, which do provide amazing instant communication opportunities. However, there is still a great advantage to face-to-face contact when it comes to conducting a membership drive. There is a great advantage to an individual personally talking to another individual about joining a membership association. The personal contact, especially when you are asking for dues or a time and energy commitment, is of paramount importance. This is not to say we shouldn't use social media, or even email, to provide materials to an individual in advance of meeting with them, or to give them background information on the association. Social media and all of our electronic communications provide a tremendous advantage in that regard. The fact remains that asking someone to join an organization should be done as a personal approach. The real key to success is the word "ask." I've heard individuals say that they don't know anyone who wants to join, but in reality, they have not asked, and that's the hard part for the volunteer leader or staff member. If nothing else resonates in this chapter, let this be the one thing: you have to ask someone to join before they will join, and it is best done personally. You must be sincere and believe in the organization yourself when talking to the prospective member. You need to be prepared before you ask someone to join the organization.

It is incumbent upon the volunteer leader or staff member participating in the membership drive to be ready with tangible, legitimate, excellent reasons why it is important for the person they are addressing to join the organization. People join for social reasons as well, and that still has real value today. As I said earlier, people with like interests join associations. They do this to accomplish goals together that they otherwise may not be able to accomplish by themselves. While the social aspects do have value for many people, in today's world, you must be able to show a potential member why it is an advantage to them to invest their time and energy in the organization. Why does it make sense for them? Also, will their time and energy be used in a valuable fashion that benefits the mission and goals of the organization, and will it also benefit them? If you can prepare for this discussion before talking to a prospective member, it is quite likely you will be successful signing that person. Think about the word "value." In the first thirty seconds to one minute of your conversation with a potential member, you must explain who you are, why you consider it important to be part of the association, and what is in it for them. This may mean information or financial gain of some type, but joining the organization must have direct value to the prospective member, or they will not join. Unfortunately, patience is a disappearing trait for lots of reasons, given the way we all live today.

Today, attention spans are vastly shorter than ever before. As a matter of fact, attention spans are almost nonexistent. We have our electronic, instant communication and social media. Being of a generation that has been more longwinded and more interested in explaining a situation with details, I fully recognize this change.

It's not always a change for the better because sometimes it takes time and detail to provide someone a proper understanding of a concept or a request. Having said that, it doesn't make any difference; the fact is that attention spans are much shorter today, and you must make your point with confidence, in a strong and respectful manner, in about thirty seconds—because after that, it is probable the prospective member will stop listening. Again, this is why preparation and practice before talking to a prospective member is important.

Let's talk a bit about one of my favorite subjects (and you know this if you have read my other books), and that is human nature. Obviously, human nature affects what we do and how we do it, including how we interpret things and react to situations. From the perspective of the individual looking to sign a prospective member, you need to understand (without criticizing anyone in any way) that human nature suggests that when you approach a potential member, you already have a challenge. That person knows you want something—in this case, dues and maybe even time. Body language is so important. As you approach a prospective member, don't look at the ground or walk up to them with your head hanging. Stand upright, go talk to the person, and look them in the eye. Eye contact is extremely important. This is hard for a lot of people to do, but eye contact indicates sincerity and conveys your belief in what you are saying. In other words, start right out with, "Hey, Joe. I need to talk to you about joining the association, and I don't want to take a lot of your time, but can you give me a minute?" Start that way and see what happens. You've already told Joe you recognize he has only so much time and that you believe in what you are about to say. Joe may even feel like you may be prepared for that discussion since you approached him with some confidence in a forthright manner. Don't apologize for anything. Talk about why you are involved in the organization and the value it will have to Joe. Don't beat around the bush. Go straight to what you want to say and respect the time of your prospective member. Respect their ability to understand what you are saying. Never patronize the prospective member. Don't beg the prospective member. The prospect needs to want to belong because it makes sense for them. They need to understand how you feel about the organization and that you are committed to your opinion.

Of course, this is easier for some personality types than others. However, if you need to practice on somebody before you visit with potential members, then do so. There is nothing wrong with that.

Thoughts for Associations

By the same token, there is a fine line here to operate within. You must be respectful of the individual you are approaching and not overbearing. Don't be demanding. There is a difference between being overbearing or demanding and being confident in what you are saying. That confidence comes through in your tone and facial expression. If the prospective member doesn't want to join the association, then they won't want to join. Don't let that bother you. If that is the case, you need to ask if you can leave some information with them and perhaps call on them at another time. If you can tell they are not going to join no matter what you say, then end the conversation.

If you feel like they have any level of interest, have your membership application ready and see if you can sign them up at that moment. There will never be a better time to sign that person up than the moment you are addressing them. Most likely, if you let them think about it and you walk away, you will be forgotten. It's a lot easier for someone to say no if you're not looking at them. But you don't want to be a pest. You want to be the individual who believes in what you are asking them to do, and you want to show your professionalism and your belief in that regard.

Do not underestimate the importance of your approach, your body language, and how you express yourself.

These are just some fundamental thoughts about the mechanics of human nature as we engage in conversation in this specific area of asking someone to join an association.

Let's ask ourselves this question, "Who has the best chance of signing the new member?" Oftentimes, it is easy to give this assignment to a paid employee, and certainly staff should assist with membership drives. They can participate and should possess the expertise to assist leaders and members in membership-drive activities. It is the responsibility—and not only that, should be the expectation—of staff to provide materials and information to help leaders and members move forward in a successful membership drive. There is no one who has more power and ability to successfully conduct a membership drive than a current member or leader in the association, whether this be a board member or committee member. Leaders are participating because they believe in the association. They are sincere about their commitment. This gives them a leg up when addressing a prospective member. This makes them a far more powerful individual to conduct a membership drive than any staff person. When leaders or current members approach a prospective member, it heightens the credibility of asking that individual to join. There is no doubt about this, and it has been true as long as there have been membership drives. In addition, leaders and members need to approach the prospective member in the confident and courteous manner described earlier. If that member or leader is well-known and well respected (which is most likely the case), it makes that individual even more powerful in regard to asking an individual to join.

What are the tools needed to successfully conduct a membership drive? We have already talked about the best people to conduct the drive, and we've talked about how to approach a potential member, but what are the other tools needed? I mentioned earlier in order to sign someone up in an association, you need to address the valued use of their time and show the potential member the advantage of joining financially. That's not always easy to do because, oftentimes, membership associations are very successful in programs or services that benefit everyone in a certain sector, whether those people belong to the organization or not. This is why the leader approaching the prospective member

must have the fortitude to talk about the importance of everyone in that sector (whether it be an appliance dealer's association, an agricultural association, or other professional group) participating in and supporting the mission of the association.

One of the most disheartening things I heard from potential members was, "Why should I get involved and pay your dues when I'm getting the advantage of what you're doing anyway?" That can be a difficult comment to deal with, yet it is not uncommon to hear that remark. Some potential members have the fortitude to say that, and while others may not say it, they may be thinking it. We need to go into these discussions with our eyes open, understanding the person we are trying to sign up may be thinking exactly that thought. Therefore, one of the first tools is being prepared to explain why there is strength in numbers in an association and why that person needs to belong to support the goals, programs, and services of the organization to benefit its members. Do not be afraid to point out the need for people to work together for an association to be successful. You can do this in a respectful manner, but do not be afraid to bring it up. Some leaders and members participating in membership drives are reluctant to point this out, especially if the prospective member has the fortitude to bring this up during the conversation. Remember the organization is successful because people belong to it, and those conducting membership drives should not be afraid to point this out in a professional and courteous manner to a potential member.

It is very important to show tangible benefits. Some of you may say, "Well, my organization does all kinds of great things, but they are subjective, and not very many of those are tangible." I would challenge you to check the list of accomplishments for your association because, often, you can correctly attach tangible value in a legitimate fashion to a great many activities and programs in a membership association. Use yourself as an example. I suggest (and I have put this into practice myself) preparing a list of advantages of belonging to the organization and taking that along when addressing a potential member. The list should be relevant and practical. For example, list activities that have provided a direct financial benefit or other benefit that helped you be successful. If the organization has conducted activities that have been of financial benefit to you, list those, using yourself as an example and how much financial benefit there was. Perhaps your organization has a discount program for members that, in itself, would pay the dues for a year. Perhaps your organization has effectively impacted legislation in areas that have saved members money or red tape. If that is the case, these activities and the financial value of those activities should be listed. At any rate, you get the picture. Before you approach a prospective member, you must be armed with information showing the practical, tangible benefits and real value of being a member, beyond the cost of dues. In other words, if you want to be effective in signing that new member, you need to be able to show them they get far more than their dues money back in benefit and value.

There is another approach that can be used on its own or in addition to the approach just mentioned—that of the initial sign-up benefit. More than one organization has successfully offered a one-time incentive to members to sign up. Old news, right? Call it a bonus to the new member for signing. In other words, you can offer new members some type of gift bag or special discount program, or funding for some products, for example, in order to secure their first annual dues payment and sign them up. This "loss leader" approach has been used by many membership organizations and can be somewhat successful. If you use this approach, you need to be totally aware of a couple facts. First of all, it is possible that some of those people you sign may not renew unless you have done a fantastic job over their first year explaining the benefits of the association beyond the initial sign-up package, or unless they have become involved, which is the best way to retain members. Perhaps your organization can live with this; perhaps not. Up to you. Many associations and businesses do this and understand the concept, and it doesn't bother them. As a matter of fact, some of those associations go right back to those same members who canceled after the first year with the same deal again. The other concept that we need to understand is, if you use this approach, you are going to spend association money to acquire a certain number of new members. This expense is something you need to budget for, and the association board needs to have a comfort level with this approach before proceeding. Not everyone likes this approach, even though it does have a degree of success. This approach is far more common in corporate business than in membership associations.

I knew of a membership association that had forty-five-dollar annual dues and offered new members a grocery certificate of greater than dues value for signing up. This is a good example of what I am talking about. The retention rate for new members who used that program was about 45 percent, and that particular association accepted that fact. Other organizations or associations may not like this approach. Even if you use this loss leader approach to sign your first-year members, you should make sure these members receive information on all programs and services of the association and the value those have for members—the real value. In addition, you should make sure (regardless of the method you use to sign new members) that members receive information about ways they can become involved in specific areas of the organization. In my other books, I discuss member involvement and using social media and electronic communications to our advantage, which is important. As I stated earlier, attention spans are shorter or nonexistent today, and we can use our amazing electronic media to our advantage. Having said that, it is important to provide new members information in a brief, efficient manner that says, "Here are several ways you can be involved in the organization, if you desire." If you provide new members this information, there needs to be either an electronic or personal contact made with the new member within two weeks after they signed up to see if they are interested in involvement. You should not be pushy in that contact, but do your follow-up to see if there is any interest in involvement. Show the new member you care. That not only gets new people involved and brings new ideas, but it also makes a statement that you (as a current member or leader) are genuinely interested in their involvement and what they think. This is very important and is not done often enough.

As we consider tools we want to use for approaching a new member, we need to have the following:

- a member benefit sheet showing tangible, financial advantages for belonging to the organization (perhaps based on your own experience), showing value beyond the cost of dues
- information you can provide to the new member, showing involvement opportunities and why their involvement is needed and would be good
- documentation of when the member was originally signed to ensure you or someone else (preferably you, if you signed the individual up) follows up with that individual about member involvement

One of the biggest mistakes associations make with new members is forgetting about them for a year, until it's time to collect dues again. We want new members to know we care about them and what they think. We want them to recognize the value of their membership and being involved. This is fundamental because people want to be cared about, and they want to know someone in the association is interested in what they think. This is not hard to do, but it does take effort. I would suggest this follow-up not be done with a postcard or a letter. It would be great if the individual who signed the new member took the initiative to call or see that person, or at least sent them an electronic message asking

that person about member-involvement opportunities they might be considering, or perhaps, just to field any questions they might have. I cannot emphasize how important that follow-up is to new members, especially regarding member retention.

As I wrap up these fundamental thoughts about membership drives, take the challenge to make sure your association does these things. If you have gained even two or three thoughts that may assist your association in the best way to design and prepare for a membership drive, then the chapter has been valuable. My thoughts turn to a conversation I used to have with a colleague of mine many years ago, pertaining to membership drives. I was fairly new to association work at that time, and he had several years of experience. He always talked about conducting the "flying wedge" approach to a membership drive, and as I think about it, he was ahead of his time. The flying wedge membership drive refers to a group of association members and leaders that divide up a territory for a membership drive to personally contact prospective members. They believed in what they were doing and had confidence, which showed as they visited potential members. They called the program a flying wedge because they literally gathered and prepared materials they would take with them to use in talking with potential members. They often started with a breakfast and then fanned out in teams of one or two to cover a predetermined territory. Most of these association members and leaders already knew who the potential members were, or they could check the membership status.

Of course, one of the things that is vastly different today is the need to make appointments with people to discuss membership. The old flying wedge worked, especially in the agricultural community, where I did association work, because someone was usually at home or around the farm every day. Today, that is not the case. But it demonstrates a preparedness, commitment, and team approach to contacting potential members. As stated earlier, both partners are probably working and, therefore, not at home during the day, so one of the challenges to personal contact today might be the need to make an appointment to see someone or just ask when they might be home. Those conducting the flying wedge in those days long ago would take materials with them (today, these could be electronic, of course), showing value of the association and also providing member-involvement information. Does it all sound familiar? Maybe we should recall from our roots the understanding that personal contact by those who truly believe in and lead the association is very powerful when it comes to a membership drive. Don't get me wrong. Use your electronic media to send materials and provide information, make appointments, and do follow-up work, and if you can sign up a new member that way, great. Give them that opportunity. However, be ready and prepared to go see the person. And if you feel you want to try a flying wedge, go for it!

Thoughts for Associations

I conclude where I started: the most important things are being prepared, believing in what you are doing, and asking a prospective member to join. May you all have successful membership drives, and remember, it takes work and time to prepare for and conduct a successful membership drive. Go for it! Charge!

Chapter 6

Communicating Effectively with People—Just Thoughts

How can we work together effectively? Let's share some basic thoughts about challenges we face as we work together. Before that, let's recognize that, thankfully, we are all different. If this was not the case, I am sure things would be far more difficult, and we would lack a tremendous amount of ingenuity, creativity, and any number of other characteristics leading to accomplishment. We need to recognize and also appreciate our

differences to work together effectively. We need to embrace the fact that people are different, and that in itself may be one of our greatest fundamental challenges. Obviously, people have different opinions and a right to express those opinions. This is not always well received by someone of a different opinion, yet that feeling of disappointment, anger, or fear at an opinion we may not agree with, or even be scared of, is something we need to understand and respect. I'm not saying you need to agree with someone else's opinion, but we need to respect that they can have a different opinion. I want to be clear that, for this book, I am not talking about opinions pertaining to legal or illegal, or moral or immoral issues. The purpose of this chapter relates to association-management business.

Let's identify a few ways we are different and, in that regard, compile a list of subjects, characteristics, or opinions that challenge our ability to effectively work together and that we must deal with in a mature and professional manner to move forward. We were all raised differently by our parents, stepparents, or guardians who, no doubt, applied their values and opinions to our upbringing. So, we usually (not always) reflect the values and opinions of those who raised us. It has been my observation this is something parents take a great deal of pride in. I think that is great. Parents have a big responsibility, and anyone raising children has a huge job to instill quality characteristics and help their children grow and develop in an excellent manner. This is a vastly important and complex assignment.

So, we are a product of our environment, and we were all raised, to some degree, in a different environment. Yes, many of those environments may be similar, but every household is different in regard to values and opinions that parents or guardians instill in their children. For example, we obviously have different political views, and most people feel quite strongly about their political views. For that matter, almost everybody feels very strongly about everything I am going to note in this chapter. And that speaks to my exact point: we must recognize the areas we are different in as we endeavor to work together. To be honest, even to some degree, our definition of right and wrong may vary, depending on how we were raised, the values we were taught, and what the actual subject is that we want to apply a right-or-wrong analysis to. We were all raised differently when it comes to being liberal, conservative, moderates, or a combination. We were all raised differently (whether we like the use of the word or not) with different prejudices, and this does not only refer to those prejudices that may come to mind immediately but also prejudices about all kinds of social and economic issues, as well as issues of the day that stem from the values and opinions we were taught as we were raised.

All of these are differences that human beings greatly value, and differences—we generally agree—are individual choices people have a right to exercise. We fundamentally believe that people have a right to exercise those differences, beliefs, and choices as long as there is no infringement upon other people who think differently or possess a difference of opinion. It takes strength of character to recognize these facts and, more importantly, to deal with these differences in an effective and fair manner. Too often, human nature interferes with this being done well. The question, therefore, is, can we respect these differences?

Mark E. Frels, CAE (Ret.)

I happen to like movies, like millions of other moviegoers. In the 1995 movie *The American President*, Michael Douglas, acting as president of the United States at a press conference, states (scene 30): "America is advanced citizenship—you've got to want it bad, 'cause it's gonna put up a fight. It's gonna say, you want free speech—let's see you acknowledge a man, whose words make your blood boil, standing center stage and advocating at the top of his lungs that which you would spend a lifetime opposing at the top of yours."

A very dramatic statement, as part of a longer speech, but lines I think about often. I think about these lines regarding this truly great country we live in and, more fundamentally, how these words apply to each and every one of us working together, debating, collaborating, and, hopefully, moving forward in our society.

So, our differences and all this obvious philosophy and commentary boils down to the need for us to understand we are different, and even though our ideas may be different, working together is so fundamentally important.

Before you begin working with someone at a meeting or on a project, give yourself the advantage of learning as much as you can about the individual or group you are going to work with, even if you think you know the person or group. As you work with colleagues or collaborate with new people, give yourself the benefit of understanding where the people you are working with are coming from in regard to philosophy, background, and so on. It is important to understand their experiences that shape their backgrounds before you try to work with them and respectfully and correctly establish your communications and provide your opinions. You certainly don't want to insult someone you are trying to work with, and by the same token, you want to effectively make your points with those individuals or the group. Understand who these people are so you can understand how to best communicate and work with them.

Another important point is that every word you choose to use in each and every sentence you say is very important. Of course, it is important for you to correctly convey your idea or comment, and, most likely, we all think about that. However, we should also think about, with the same level of consideration, how the words we choose will be received. This is the part most people don't pay enough attention to, either because they don't think about it or don't care, or perhaps they just feel that the other person can figure it out for themselves. We all know one word can change the entire meaning of a sentence. When you give consideration to your remarks in a detailed fashion, before making those remarks to hopefully accurately convey your thoughts, it takes considerable thought. It takes work and training to think this way before you speak. Again, I am not indicating you change your thoughts—only how you present your thoughts.

This becomes a customized and personal approach to communicating with groups or each individual. It is possible you already know what the person you are communicating with wants to hear or how they feel about a subject. So, as you try to make your point, how do you proceed so you will be clearly understood, given their background and experiences?

What is it you want to achieve by communicating with that person? In other words, your communication style, verbal or written, with each individual or group, can and should vary, depending upon how you want your words and thoughts to be received. This takes work—a lot of work if done correctly—but it pays off in increased, clear understanding and excellent communication.

Another point is, after you convey your thoughts to an individual or the group, can you receive their thoughts in an equal fashion? You should be allowed to make your points in a discussion, as should the person or group you are communicating with. The question is, can you give them a fair and equal turn to communicate? Can you allow them to make their points in that discussion as well? Can you do so without becoming emotional, depending upon the subject? We all know this can be difficult, especially if the subject matter is considered personal or emotional or otherwise subjective in some manner. Can you allow yourself to engage in an equal and fair exchange of ideas even when those ideas are the opposite of yours? Once again, you certainly do not need to agree with those ideas, and you can reject ideas. That is your right, as it is the right of the individual or group you are talking to. But can you listen to those ideas and understand where that person or group is coming from so you can respond? When you do respond, can you choose correct and appropriate words, important to expressing your opinion, that will be received correctly by the individual or group?

Another point to consider is an old concept that has been around for a long time and is extremely important. It's the concept of listening. This concept has undergone real challenges in recent years. I believe most people will tell you they believe listening is important, but sometimes we don't do it very well anymore, especially today. Social media, email, and texting have provided great immediate communication advantages. I am a user of these technologies because of the vast efficiency in time, energy, and cost. However, the training that comes with use of these electronic tools, in the area of brevity, presents a real challenge. We live in a world of one-word or one-phrase answers, and no one seems to have time to read a paragraph. As I have noted in other books, sometimes it takes five or six lines (or more) to adequately explain a situation or question. I am not only talking about the written word but also effective conversation and listening.

My point is that the brevity of today's communications can cause challenges, especially as you strive to work with a person or group on program development, an issue, or whatever the topic may be. Many people struggle with listening because it takes time and effort. It seems we all have a hundred things to do every hour. We are busy, we want to get things done, and we live in a cut-to-the-chase society when it comes to talking with someone. We say we don't like repetition and someone reminding us about something several times. Yet, time and again, those reminders are needed, and perhaps we didn't do exactly what we thought we were going to do on a program or issue because we didn't totally understand the description of the project or assignment. Why? Maybe because we did not listen or communicate long enough to understand the assignment. The point is that listening and complete communications are important. We live in a society of instant communication, and this has had a challenging effect on the art of listening, sharing ideas, and discussing concepts, which are so important to collaboration and understanding what another person wants to convey. I understand the discontent with repetition or long discussions, and somewhere there has to be a happy medium. However, points must be communicated clearly with whatever medium we choose to utilize.

Generally, people like to be listened to. Employees like supervisors and other employees to hear their ideas. As I noted in my second book, someone may not get what they want out of a meeting, but if you give them time to express their ideas and concepts, they may consider that meeting a success. People like to be listened to and don't like to be cut off when trying to make a point. One of the trends I have noticed in recent years (which is very disturbing) is people being cut off by someone else. Sometimes when two people are engaging in a conversation

Thoughts for Associations

and one person becomes disinterested in what the other is saying, that person simply walks off or turns away. How rude is that? I would prefer the individual who is disinterested say to the person talking something like "I appreciate those points and let's visit that again someday," or if they aren't interested, "Would you excuse me?" While those actions wouldn't be very well received by the individual talking, there is also a need to be fair in this situation. You can't listen to somebody talk for an hour, saying the same thing ten times or talking about something you don't care about. But, by the same token, the minute someone says something you don't care about or are disinterested in, it's not fair to just rudely look the other way and start a conversation with someone else or walk off. I've seen this happen, I don't know how many times, especially in recent years. Don't just cut people off or walk away when they are trying to make a point. You owe it to that person to listen to them and to give them your fair and honest opinion with respect. If you don't like what they are saying, tell them you don't like it in a respectful manner. That allows them to have their opinion and allows you to have your opinion as well. Can we handle that kind of honest and mature communication? I'm not sure. Or is it just easier to walk off or make up an excuse? But then the subject comes up over and over again in the future because we haven't communicated fairly and effectively about that subject.

Respect the other person's thoughts and take time to listen to them at least for a while. They should take time to listen to you as well. Listening can be difficult, especially if what the person is saying is emotionally or personally challenging to you. Brevity is fine, but there are times we need to listen to one another a little longer to understand, at least within a reasonable time frame—whatever that may be—what the other person is saying. As with all things, I suspect being reasonable and utilizing some moderation is important and the key to success.

Another aspect of communicating and working with people is

recognition. I have talked about this in other publications to a greater detail, so I won't dwell on it in this book, other than to say that effectively working with people requires recognition. If someone should be recognized for doing a good job, it is important to do so in the correct manner that fits the action. It's important for supervisors to lead and provide direction in a clear manner so people can effectively move forward, understanding assignments they have been given. When people don't achieve objectives they have been given, this should be pointed out privately, and actions should be taken to correct those issues. Recognition is important to collaboration, motivation, and instilling enthusiasm in anyone you work with, especially when you have reached a successful outcome and your objectives. Don't forget to say thank you to people, and don't forget to recognize people.

These are just a few thoughts about working with people. Hopefully, there have been some basic thoughts or comments in this chapter that cause you to think about these points as you prepare for your next staff meeting, prepare to work with an outside consultant, or engage in a verbal discussion or debate with a colleague. We all have thoughts, and all we need to do to effectively collaborate in a positive fashion is respect one another's opinions and communicate completely and clearly with respect. Can we do that? It takes thought, maturity, respect, and effort.

Chapter 7

Dedication

How do we define dedication? I suspect we all have our own definition of being dedicated to something, whether it is our family or job or an objective. Defining dedication is a somewhat subjective challenge we face. We know that being dedicated to your family and job is extremely important. It is important to also be dedicated to your principles and your values, and those vary with all of us, depending upon our opinions, backgrounds, and a multitude of factors. For the purposes of this chapter, we will be, of course, defining dedication pertaining to association management and the employment environment today. Dedication is also defined by your priorities and judgment. I suspect most people feel they are, indeed, dedicated to their family first and to their job or employment duties. But I submit there is a wide variance between people and their definitions of dedication. This chapter is designed to cause you to think about your definition of dedication and what it means to you. My definition of dedication can be different from yours or someone else's.

As we look at the definition of being dedicated, there are several key words that come to mind. All of these factor into our individual definitions of dedication. These words are commitment, priorities, sacrifice, organization, planning or working ahead, loyalty, results, and the phrase *you and your employer*.

First, let's talk about commitment. If you are committed to something, in my book, this means you are absolutely on board

with making sure the task you have been assigned is going to be achieved in a successful manner. If you are committed to something, that means you are 100 percent on board with making sure you do all you can to be successful. If you say you are going to do something, you should do it and do it with your best effort. If you are committed, you are making a statement about your actions, and others will watch as you proceed to fulfill your commitment. There's a key word. If you are committed to something, you are *obligated* to fulfill that commitment within the time frame prescribed. I'm not sure there is a lot of variance to define the word commitment because you are either committed to something or not. Commitment is a key factor in being dedicated.

If you say you are going to be somewhere at 8:00 a.m., are you there at 8:00 a.m.? And to make sure that is the case, have you planned in such a manner that you have allowed for contingencies that may cause you to be late? Commitment means you are willing to do what it takes to achieve the goal or task.

Having priorities can be challenging. I believe we can all agree, and certainly should, that family comes first. Being dedicated to your family is number one. I think most of us were probably raised that way. But how does the word "priorities" fit into our discussion about being dedicated to our job? The definition of being dedicated to a job or to your employer, I think, has changed significantly over the last several years. When I began my career, we were all thrilled to get a job. We wanted to work and wanted our employer to know that they were a priority. I will readily admit to sometimes missing other nonwork events or activities that I probably should not have missed because my priority was my employer. Many of you can say the same. I suppose there is a happy medium somewhere, which is often the case, and we need to recognize that moderation in all things is good. I did not take, by my choice, lots of vacation time, to say the least. But by the same token, I was dedicated to my employer and was proud of that. I enjoyed what I did for a living. I grew up in an environment where my mother, who is an extremely accomplished, professional woman, was always very dedicated to her career, and my father, who was a farmer, was always very dedicated to the farm. Both of them were tremendous role models and examples to me of being dedicated and committed but also keeping their priorities straight. They certainly did that and offered good lessons. But in order to have some balance in our life, we need to consider our priorities. Employers want to know employees are dedicated to the company that is paying them wages and benefits. So, as you think about your priorities and about being dedicated to your employer, what are your priorities for making sure you reach the goals your employer has put before you? Are you able to make your employment a priority in your life?

Sacrifice is an interesting word. Simply put, are you willing to give up some things to advance your career? Not everyone is willing to do this. One of the most common examples of sacrificing to move your career forward has to do with relocation. Throughout my career, I relocated several times for employment opportunities that advanced my career and my desire to serve the association in new and exciting ways. Lots of people I have known have been unable or unwilling to relocate, and that has limited their growth and development in the association. Relocating involves sacrifice, especially if you are rooted in a community or if you have children in school. Relocating, as everyone reading this book knows, can be traumatic and upsetting, and—don't get me wrong—relocating may not be possible for you for a variety of reasons, but it is often a factor in advancement. Today, with more work-at-home options, it can sometimes be addressed, but that is not always the case. It depends on the job.

There are other sacrifices as well, such as the sacrifice of time and energy. Earlier, I talked about priorities and the fact that family is a priority for all of us, but we need to analyze our priorities after family to decide where our employment fits in our overall list of priorities. So, are you willing or able to sacrifice some of your extra time in order to make your employer more successful and, possibly, to advance your career? Many of you are already doing this, but not everyone can answer that question, "Yes." Are you willing to go the extra mile and set aside your own personal goals or desires for the good of the company and your employment? Not everyone is willing to do that, but I submit to you that employees who follow this path will and should be rewarded for those efforts. We need to remember that it takes hard work and effort to advance a career, and it takes hard work and effort to move forward and accomplish tasks and assignments in a successful, professional manner.

Another aspect of being dedicated is being an organized employee. Are you organized in your employment habits, or do you, as my generation would say, "Fly by the seat of your pants?" My tendency is to plan, sometimes possibly too far ahead, but I would rather do that and make adjustments when needed regarding events or activities, or whatever the case may be, than wait until the last minute. If you look at the components of being a dedicated employee, believe me that procrastination is not a component or a quality that any employer is looking for. Procrastination is a

real enemy of success and of being an organized and dedicated employee. Don't just use your calendar to only remind you of meetings and phone calls; use your calendar to help you plan ahead with regard to deadlines and activities that need to be accomplished. You will be a better, more dedicated, and organized employee if you keep lists and cross off your accomplishments each day and then make a new list so you are ready to go tomorrow. You will be a better employee if you work ahead in regard to planning, at least on major activities or functions.

Another aspect of being an organized employee is dealing with details. I can tell you, especially in association management, that success is often found in the details. Lots of people like to be big-picture folks and come up with an idea, launch that idea, and then walk away, and while ideas are always needed, the detail work also has to get done. Somebody has to do that detail work, especially in association management where we deal with programs, leadership development, and lots of other people-oriented activities. In order to do that, you must be organized and work ahead. Whether or not an event, new program, or activity is successful, is often found in whether or not you, as an association employee, have paid attention to every detail, prepared for every contingency, and checked and double-checked those details. The old saying, the devil is in the details, is correct, especially when it comes to planning and carrying out successful association programs.

I have talked about loyalty in my other books. I'm sure that from time to time as people have read those books, there have been some sneers. Loyalty in an employee is extremely important. I am not talking about blind loyalty where you never express your opinion or just agree with everything. I am talking about being loyal to the mission of the organization, being a team player, and being an employee who puts your best ideas forward, always, in a collaborative fashion with other employees and in a professional, courteous approach. You should always have the best interest of the company at hand. This is huge, and it factors into the definition of dedication. It is a trait that is a must in any employee who is dedicated. I think loyalty, to some degree, is self-explanatory. Don't make fun of other employees and don't gossip. Carry forward the mission of the association in a proud manner at all times.

It is important to understand that loyalty to the company does not mean you sacrifice being your own person or your own thoughts

but rather that you bring forward the best of your thoughts in a professional manner. It also means you represent the company not only when you are at work but also when you are not at work. This is a concept that has seen some dramatic change in the last several years. When you are not at work, especially if you are in a public office or an association-management position, you are still on display. This is a difficult concept for a lot of people to accept. If you are the manager of X association on Monday through Friday, you are still the manager of X association when you are at the grocery store or your kid's ballgame on the weekend. This is a concept of being professional we need to continue to embrace. It is not to say, by any stroke of the imagination, that you don't have a right to your own life, as most certainly you do. But we need to understand you are still viewed as the manager of your association, or the program director of your organization, whether it be Saturday, Sunday, or Wednesday night. There is a responsibility that comes with that, and it ties back to loyalty and commitment. It ties back to being loyal to the company and conducting yourself in a manner that is acceptable to your position and respectful to your employer.

Achieving results is another aspect of being a dedicated employee. Do you meet objectives you have been given? Do you achieve your results on time or maybe even early? Sometimes it is very difficult to achieve the results. I believe most employers, even if results are not completely achieved because of circumstances, will understand if the dedicated employee has done everything possible to achieve results. Let's hope that most of the time the achievement of results is, in fact, the greatest earmark of the dedicated employee. But it is not just achieving the results; it's also how we get from point A to point B to achieve those results. Have you done this in a correct and professional manner?

The last area I want to comment on in this chapter is what I call "you and the company." What is the relationship between you and your employer? Certainly, it should be a two-way street. I want to make that clear. You should be loyal, committed, willing to make some sacrifices, results-oriented, and work in the best interest of your employer. Your employer has a right to expect that from you. You have a right to expect that your employer will see you as an excellent employee and, perhaps, reward you for your efforts when you are successful. Certainly, being rewarded for your success comes within the ability of the company to do so, based on resources available. The place to foster that relationship and display the characteristics and traits we have talked about in this chapter is between you as the dedicated employee and your supervisor.

I believe if you conduct yourself as a dedicated employee in the manner we have discussed in this chapter,

you will find that your association will appreciate your efforts. You will find you have a career and not just a job. You will find, I believe, an increased degree of self-satisfaction in what you are doing for your career. These are concepts we need to remember as we work in any job and especially as we work in association management. Associations exist because people can do together what, perhaps, they cannot do individually. They exist because people with like interests want to get together and make a difference for their industry or area of business. They exist for the sake of professional collaboration to achieve results, and this is what makes association management so important and interesting.

As you think about what it means to be a dedicated association employee, ask yourself how you conduct yourself as an employee. What kind of relationship do you have with your association? I hope it is a great relationship, consisting of respect back and forth. If that is the case, you will be a successful employee, and your association will be successful because of your efforts as well as the efforts of other employees and the leaders who are so important to our association process. Be that dedicated employee and move forward with confidence. May all the success come to you! I challenge you to enjoy your association work and find satisfaction in your efforts.

Chapter 8

So You Want to Be a Leader

There are elected leaders and those who serve in a staff leadership role. If you are interested in becoming a leader, first you must be passionate about the position you want to pursue, to the point of committing your most valuable resources—time, energy, and talent.

First and foremost is honestly assessing your interest. It is important you have a personal comfort level with why you are seeking the position and that you embrace the characteristics of being a leader (staff or elected) that go with the position. It is expected you feel strongly about the abilities you bring to the position along with dedication and talent. It is assumed (and should be) that you have no personal agenda or ax to grind that is motivating your desire for the position. You should genuinely desire to improve the association you want to serve. These are all self-analysis questions that anyone seeking to be a leader must ask themselves. After answering these questions, it would seem reasonable for an individual to move on to the next step in the process.

The next step is putting yourself forward. If you are a staff person looking to advance, this should be evident by your accomplishments and enthusiasm. Have you made yourself, via your actions, dedication, and work ethic, an excellent choice for promotion? Have you shown interest in that position and made your wishes known to your supervisor? This does not guarantee such a position, but that approach, along with proper training and an excellent work record are certainly steps in the right direction. For a leadership person, the same concepts apply. Have you worked your way up in the organization and accepted various responsibilities and leadership roles? Have you grown and developed in those roles? Is it obvious your talents, abilities, and experience make you a viable candidate for a future, larger leadership role? Regardless of whether it is a staff or elected leadership position, you don't start at the top. Too many people want to be propelled immediately to the top. You need to work your way toward the top and do so in an ethical, professional manner. Remember, while these are obvious, important, fundamental steps, there are no guarantees for a variety of reasons. Perhaps, the words "diligence," "patience," and "drive" are also most important to remember.

There is another fundamental consideration that is important. Let's say you aspire to a leadership position or advancement as a staff leader, and the time comes for you to be considered.

In order to advance, you must say yes to that advancement. You must say yes and agree to the challenges and commitment that comes with being a leader. Oftentimes, people who don't get leadership positions wonder how other people got those positions. The people that advanced

Thoughts for Associations

to those leadership positions did their self-analysis and resolved to invest time, energy, and talent, but they also said yes when asked to serve. Not everyone says yes. Not everyone wants to. Not everyone desires to aspire to either a staff or elected leadership position. That's okay. This is an individual choice of a personal nature. You should not accept a leadership position (elected or staff) unless you are willing to do the job to your best ability. There may be a variety of reasons why you do not want to make that commitment or cannot make that commitment, and this is understandable. No one should judge your self-analysis or particular situation, which is different for everyone. Saying yes may seem extremely fundamental, but this is something only you can do after your personal considerations.

One of the challenges businesses and associations face today is more and more people who don't say yes to accepting challenges

because of other commitments. To be fair, this has changed some over the years. Many years ago, both spouses did not work, and today, that is quite often not the case, with both spouses working to make ends meet.

Families are involved in a multitude of activities involving not only mom and dad but also grandma, grandpa, and other family members. Saying yes and accepting that leadership commitment means you will lead by example and are going to carry out the mission of the organization in an honorable and ethical fashion.

There are a variety of characteristics that make up an excellent leader. I suspect most of you reading this can name those, but let's focus on ten:

1. Can you commit time, energy, and talent to fulfill duties?
2. Always act in an ethical manner.
3. Always utilize fairness in your processes dealing with people, program development, and so on.
4. Strive to exercise good judgment.
5. Be committed to following your association policies, rules, and bylaws.
6. Follow the mission of the association first and foremost above personal gain.
7. Be a role model.
8. Report correctly, whether this be to a supervisor, president of a board, or board of directors.
9. Understand and administer delegation correctly and fairly.
10. Understand and administer correct reward and reprimand procedures.

These are ten of the most fundamental characteristics needed by a leader. Maybe better put, these are not only characteristics but actions a leader must commit to. Let's take a look at each of these subjects.

When it comes to being committed, it is important to understand priorities. Family always comes first, and no one expects (I hope) anything else to be the case. However, it is important to understand that fulfilling duties means completing assignments on time, being present when you are supposed to be, and being prepared for your duties. People often take a position and think they will be committed but forget about preparation time. If you are going to conduct monthly meetings, prepare remarks, or whatever the case may be, you have to factor into your thinking time for preparation. There's a rule I use that goes with the acceptance of any leadership position. Take the time you know you will spend involved directly in leadership activities and then add another 40 percent minimum for preparation, phone calls, and everything else that will, indeed, naturally come with a leadership position. That may sound like a lot, but it is true. A leader needs to understand and accept that level of commitment. This is why it is important to have a genuine interest in the leadership position and, more importantly, a passion for that position. If you like what you are doing, your commitment of time, energy, and talent will not seem as burdensome, and you will enjoy your experience. Don't say yes to fulfilling leadership duties unless it is something you really want to do.

I was heavily committed to my various staff leadership positions throughout my career. I absolutely enjoyed going to work every day and representing the members and leaders in our association. I preferred solving problems and doing everything I could to make the organization better. I say that not to provide a commercial for what I did but because if you are going to commit to a leadership position, you will be much better off if you enjoy the work. Some of you may be reading this and saying, "Tell me something new," but you would be surprised how many people say yes and then find themselves in a leadership position but not really having a passion for the work. If you enjoy your position, it will absolutely show in your efforts.

Ethics is an interesting characteristic, but as I have stated in other publications, it's straightforward. What's the best way to define ethics? I think it is by simply asking, "Are you doing the right thing?" Ethics are not hard to follow. My advice to staff members and leadership over the years has always been as follows: if you find yourself unable to clearly determine an ethical path in a situation, don't guess—seek help. There is always help available. Taking the ethical path and making the correct choice for your association, and for you, is not something you should ever take chances with and not something that should be guessed at.

A good leader will always do an ethical analysis of a situation before making judgments.

Tying into ethics and similar in many respects is fairness. Maybe it's better stated as "being fair." This may seem like another fundamental comment, but a good leader needs to view any situation, whether it's program development, employee conflict, performance reviews, or whatever the case may be, in a fair manner. Before you make a judgment, hear all sides of an argument and make sure you are treating everyone fairly. Sometimes it is hard to avoid a conscious or an unconscious prejudice that could taint your conclusion. Weigh the issue, listen to all information, and make a fair judgment. This is not always easy. For example, in an employee conflict, it is possible you may like one employee better than the other employee for a variety of reasons. Regardless of that, it is important for you to evaluate the conflict between those employees in a fair manner. Sometimes making lists helps in this regard. I have used that approach before in regard to pros and cons of a situation that I had to evaluate and pass a judgment upon.

I think the definition of being fair is self-explanatory, but can you follow that? Can you be fair if it means, perhaps, reprimanding a favorite employee or giving up something yourself for the good of the organization? These are the real tests of being fair. Have good reasons to support your judgments and conclusions.

You might also use the word unbiased to define being fair. Being fair is not always easy as you consider personnel issues or other issues that need to be resolved. Fairness can always be found in the analysis of facts. John Adams, our second US president, stated, "Facts are stubborn things." That quotation has stuck with me over the years and seen me through many challenging decisions. It is true that facts are stubborn things and are undeniable, and an integral part of being unbiased or nonprejudiced and making a fair assessment of a situation.

The next subject is exercising good judgment. You may think being ethical and fair and exercising good judgment all go together, and they do, but they all have their individual characteristics.

How do you exercise good judgment? It's simple: you weigh all the facts in a fair and ethical manner, as has previously noted, and then exercise good judgment utilizing those tools and abilities. In other words, you exercise good judgment by being committed, ethical, and fair. Exercising good judgment is the end result of your analysis utilizing those characteristics. Exercising good judgment and putting that judgment into action is the result of your analysis. Also, you must understand there are times when confidentiality is important. There are times when transparency is also important. Confidentiality certainly has a legal and a correct place in personnel management. I don't believe I need to go into examples of personnel conflicts or performance-review situations where confidentiality is a must. Likewise, transparency also has an important place. For example, as staff or an elected leader, keeping the other staff or board of directors informed in a timely and accurate manner is extremely important. It is also important to utilize transparency, when appropriate, to keep staff informed, motivated, and engaged in the process of their work in a manner that makes them feel informed, fulfilled, and successful.

Another characteristic of leadership is even more straightforward. Are you committed to following association or business entity policies, rules, and bylaws? Are you committed to following procedures in the correct manner, as determined by policymakers, to formulate, update, delete, and add to those policies, rules, or bylaws? This is of extreme importance. Bylaws are the governing documents of an association. In many cases, bylaws relate back to board interpretation, which led to rules and policies being established after tremendous amounts of effort and time. As an elected leader or staff leader, you must be committed to following the rules and bylaws of your association. This is the same as following a constitution for your organization. To violate or change these documents without proper procedures causes more than great difficulty. There are occasions when interpretations may be necessary based on a specific situation. In the case of most associations, especially membership organizations, that interpretation lies with the board of directors. This is as it should be and is an important role the board has, along with fiduciary responsibilities and other duties. Simply put, as a leader, can you follow the rules of the organization?

Also, as a leader, you need to obviously be committed to the mission of the organization above any personal interests. Don't confuse this with ambition. Someone who has a sincere desire and passion to serve, and who would like to be a leader for those reasons, certainly should pursue those interests. Someone with those characteristics who is willing to commit should understand and support the mission of the association. As a matter of fact, it is probably the mission of the association that fostered interest in the potential leadership person to serve. What we are talking about is keeping the mission, health, and focus of the organization above your personal interests.

Once again, this is an area that should be self-explanatory but is extremely important. I submit to you that a leader will garner considerable individual growth and gain anyway through their leadership experience.

The potential leader clearly must understand that they will be a role model. This is a huge commitment. If they are a staff leader, they will be a role model for staff, and, of course, the same

goes for elected leadership so vital to the association. We should view being a role model as an opportunity for training other people. When you are a role model, you have significant influence on how people think and conduct themselves. This is a huge responsibility and one not enough people take seriously. This includes not only how you do your job and complete assignments but also how you appear, act, and conduct yourself, not only at work but also in the community. This is something that causes a challenge for a great number of people who say, "But I want a life of my own." I would submit to those people that you certainly can do that (and no one is denying that opportunity), but there is a real responsibility that comes with being a role model. It means you are on display all the time in one way or another. That is a big responsibility. Your role is a training function and is powerful because often people who have served as role models continue in that capacity long after other folks have replaced them. They are still called upon and consulted with and asked for opinions. Make sure you have a comfort level with that before deciding you want to be a leader. The commitment is not only time and energy but also a commitment regarding how you act and are perceived by others, not only at your association but by the general public.

Reporting is another aspect of being a leader. We all have reporting responsibilities. I have noticed over the last several years that reporting to a supervisor seems to be more

and more difficult for many people. Why in the world should it be difficult? An association or a company is paying you to fulfill your job, per your job description, and you have a supervisor. It seems reasonable you should keep your supervisor informed. In the case of upper management, that supervisor may be a board president or a board of directors. You can file electronic reports as appropriate, given the nature of confidentiality of information, or you can meet person to person. If you have read my other books, you will know I prefer, at least on occasion, for parties to meet face-to-face because the dynamics of that meeting are completely different from electronic reports filed once a week or biweekly. Reporting is important for order and to assess progress. It is important for the relationship between a supervisor and an employee. The same goes for elected leadership. Even an elected president of an association has an obligation to report and discuss information with the board of directors within the policies and guidelines of the particular association or organization.

Today, I hear some people say, "I really don't want to report to anybody. Just tell me what to do, and I'll go do it." I have no idea how they can accurately and correctly do that on behalf of the association without reporting to a supervisor and having some supervisor-employee communication to continue discussing goals and objectives and stay on track. If you're going to be a leader, reporting in an appropriate and correct manner is always important in order to analyze and plan for the future. It is the correct approach to organize efforts and move forward in an efficient and effective manner. Situations change from time to time, and communication is vital to making necessary adjustments.

It is very appropriate that we just talked about reporting, because now I want to comment on delegation. If we are honest, this one can be hard for all of us. In one of my other publications, I discuss the term "control freaks." I mention I really don't like that term because the truth is we are all control freaks—every one of us. I know people who have called another person a control freak, and the person making that call was much more that way than the person they were trying to label. Having said that, delegation can be difficult but necessary to utilize the best talents of staff or leaders and move forward effectively as a team. A good leader delegates to other staff or other leaders and provides them parameters under which to operate. Those parameters may be logistical or financial, and often there are budget limitations and other considerations. However, much more can be accomplished through delegation and utilizing the talents of your staff or other leaders. As a matter of fact, the good leader knows this is a must to accomplish the large programs of work that most associations have these days.

It is extremely important that reporting occurs with this delegation. Delegation without reporting won't work and hampers a coordinated effort. Not everyone will agree with that. A lot of people would like to have delegation and no reporting, and this does not serve the best interest of the entity in an efficient manner. Some people may feel the opposite is true. If you understand the value of delegation and match your assignments to people with appropriate talents and motivation, you will find your team is much more successful. Then, when delegation has been successful, you can celebrate and reward team efforts. That becomes successful teamwork, and everyone can enjoy the success.

This leads me to the final characteristic of a leader. This is the ability to reward and reprimand. As a leader, don't hesitate to thank staff or other leaders publicly. People desire to be rewarded and should be recognized when they do a good job. Likewise, when appropriate and necessary, a leader must also reprimand. Staff does this with staff, and leaders do this with leaders. Very rare is a situation where those sectors would cross. This is especially the case in the association-management world. Properly rewarded employees will move forward in a productive, collaborative fashion. When you need to reprimand, do so in private, and most of the time, this will be the correct approach.

This chapter has focused on a tremendous amount of fundamental information, but again, I ask, has the chapter made you think further about any of these aspects of being a leader? Are you considering a leadership role and need to think about these aspects? Let me leave you with this: being a leader, either elected or staff, is a tremendous experience, a true honor, and an opportunity to work with a lot of wonderful people and open doors, while furthering your own development and the best interests of the organization. If you have the commitment and passion to be a leader, I applaud you and wish you all possible success!

About the Author

Mark E. Frels, CAE (Ret) was born and raised on a multigenerational family grain and livestock farm in Rock Island County, Illinois. He is an honors graduate of Iowa Wesleyan University. Mark participated in many student organizations, including yearbook, newspaper, and varsity baseball.

Mark completed two study terms at a young age at the University of Madrid in Madrid, Spain, through the auspices of Augustana College in Rock Island, Illinois. He held an internship as a radio announcer during his college years at KILJ Radio in Mt. Pleasant, Iowa. During the summers, he was employed by the USDA Soil Conservation Service as a survey technician assistant.

Mark began full-time employment with the Illinois Farm Bureau (corporately known as the Illinois Agricultural Association) in 1977 and completed more than thirty-five years of service with that association. The Illinois Farm Bureau is the state's largest volunteer-membership association of farmers and those supporting agriculture, with approximately four hundred thousand members. It is one of the largest state Farm Bureau membership organizations in the country.

Mark began his work for Illinois Farm Bureau as a county Farm Bureau manager trainee in 1977 and, in that same year, was hired as the Knox County Farm Bureau manager in Galesburg, Illinois, a position he held for approximately ten years. Mark then moved to a regional manager position covering the northern one-third of the state, working with county Farm Bureau association boards and managers on behalf of the

Illinois Farm Bureau. Following several years as a regional manager, he became the Illinois Farm Bureau director of field services, moving to the association state headquarters in Bloomington, Illinois, to head that division. Later, he was named executive director of member services and public relations, which combined the News & Communications Division and the Field Services Division in a new corporate structure. He became a member of the Illinois Farm Bureau management team reporting directly to the president of the organization.

Mark retired in 2013 to pursue association project interests and devote more time to family and the family farm. He is a member of the Blue Key Academic Scholastic Fraternity, a 4-H Alumni award winner, and a member of 4-H Club Congress. He received the Honorary Chapter Farmer recognition from the Galesburg FFA and an Honorary State FFA degree from Illinois Association of Future Farmers of America. He is a recipient of the Knox County Farm Bureau Meritorious Service Award to Agriculture and the recipient of the Iowa Wesleyan University Distinguished Alumni Award. He holds a Certified Association Executive (CAE, ret.) designation from the American Society of Association Executives (ASAE). Throughout his career, Mark has had several management articles published in the ASAE national publication, *Associations Now*.

It is Mark's love for the organization he served, including the leaders, staff, and association members he worked with, that inspires his works, such as this book and his previous two books dealing with association management. He has published two other fundamental association-management books, *Just Common Sense* and *More Common Sense*. It is his passion for organizational work and, in particular, for communications that has been the significant driver in his desire to share fundamental association-management thoughts and concepts.

Mark and his wife, Ann, a retired high school English teacher and retired municipal employee for the town of Normal, Illinois, now live in rural Wyanet, Illinois.

www.ingramcontent.com/pod-product-compliance
Lightning Source LLC
Chambersburg PA
CBHW020445220526
45464CB00002B/863